LIGHTNING
BOLT
BOOKS™

# Explore Uranus

## Jackie Golusky

Lerner Publications • Minneapolis

**PAGE PLUS+**

**Scan the QR code on page 21 to see Uranus in 3D!**

Lerner Publications Company
An imprint of Lerner Publishing Group, Inc.
241 First Avenue North
Minneapolis, MN 55401 USA

For reading levels and more information, look up this title at www.lernerbooks.com.

Main body text set in Billy Infant regular.
Typeface provided by SparkType.

**Library of Congress Cataloging-in-Publication Data**

Names: Golusky, Jackie, 1996- author.
Title: Explore Uranus / Jackie Golusky.
Other titles: Lightning bolt books. Planet explorer.
Description: Minneapolis, MN : Lerner Publications, [2021] | Series: Lightning bolt books - Planet explorer | Includes bibliographical references and index. | Audience: Ages 6-9 | Audience: Grades 2-3 | Summary: "This cold, giant planet may be far away, but scientists know lots about it and are striving to discover even more. Learn all about Uranus and what makes it such a cool planet"— Provided by publisher.
Identifiers: LCCN 2020018804 (print) | LCCN 2020018805 (ebook) | ISBN 9781728404141 (library binding) | ISBN 9781728423661 (paperback) | ISBN 9781728418506 (ebook)
Subjects: LCSH: Uranus (Planet)—Juvenile literature.
Classification: LCC QB681 .G674 2021  (print) | LCC QB681  (ebook) | DDC 523.47—dc23

LC record available at https://lccn.loc.gov/2020018804
LC ebook record available at https://lccn.loc.gov/2020018805

Manufactured in the United States of America
2-51885-48986-10/7/2021

# Table of Contents

# All about Uranus

About 1.8 billion miles (2.9 billion km) from the sun is the cold, blue world of Uranus.

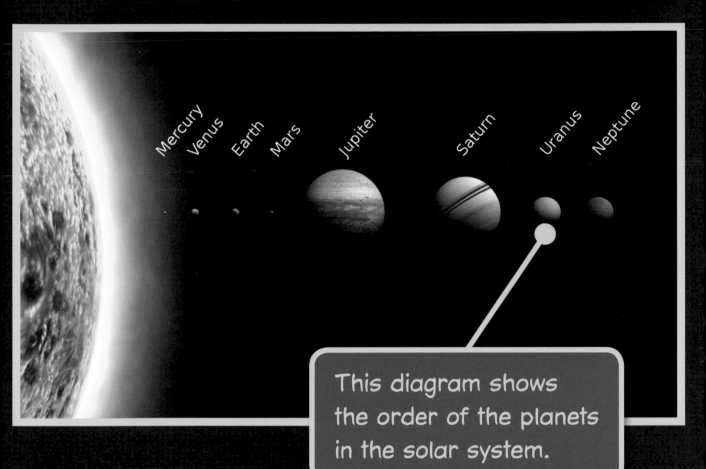

Mercury
Venus
Earth
Mars
Jupiter
Saturn
Uranus
Neptune

This diagram shows the order of the planets in the solar system.

Uranus is the seventh planet from the sun. As the second-coldest planet in the solar system, it can reach -372°F (-224°C). That's cold enough to freeze oxygen.

Uranus is about 31,518 miles (50,724 km) across. It is four times wider than Earth.

Uranus and Neptune are the last two planets in the solar system. Scientists call Uranus and Neptune ice giants because the planets are large and made of icy material.

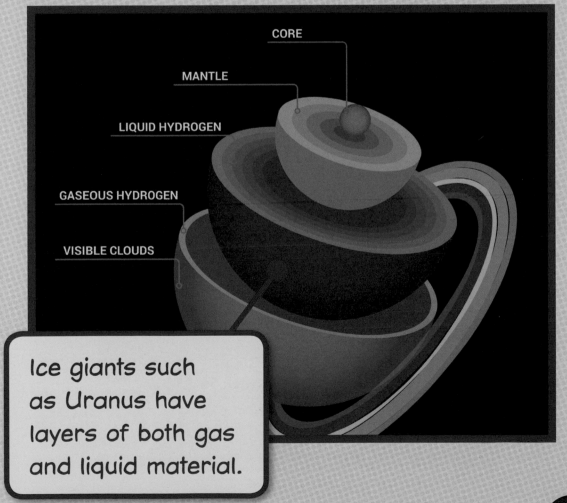

CORE

MANTLE

LIQUID HYDROGEN

GASEOUS HYDROGEN

VISIBLE CLOUDS

Ice giants such as Uranus have layers of both gas and liquid material.

# Uranus's Moons and Rings

Uranus has twenty-seven moons. Titania is the largest at 981 miles (1,579 km) across. The smallest, Cupid, is only 11 miles (18 km) across. That's smaller than New York City.

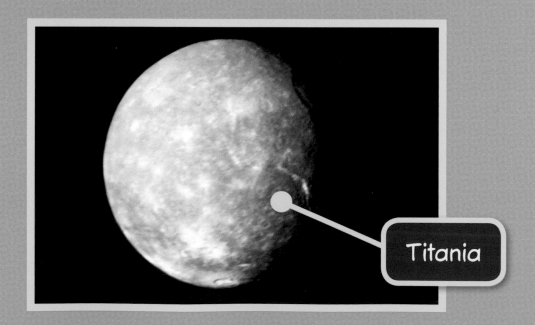

Titania

This cold, rocky land belongs to Uranus's moon Miranda.

Astronomers have seen ice on the surface of five of Uranus's moons. The ice on these moons seems to be made of dirty water. Most astronomers think the moons are too cold to support life.

Uranus's rings were discovered in 1977. An artist created this painting of the planet and its rings soon after.

Uranus has thirteen rings. These rings are made up of dust and icy rocks. The inner rings are narrow and dark, while the outer rings are wide and colorful.

Most of the outer rings are red. But Uranus's outermost ring is blue.

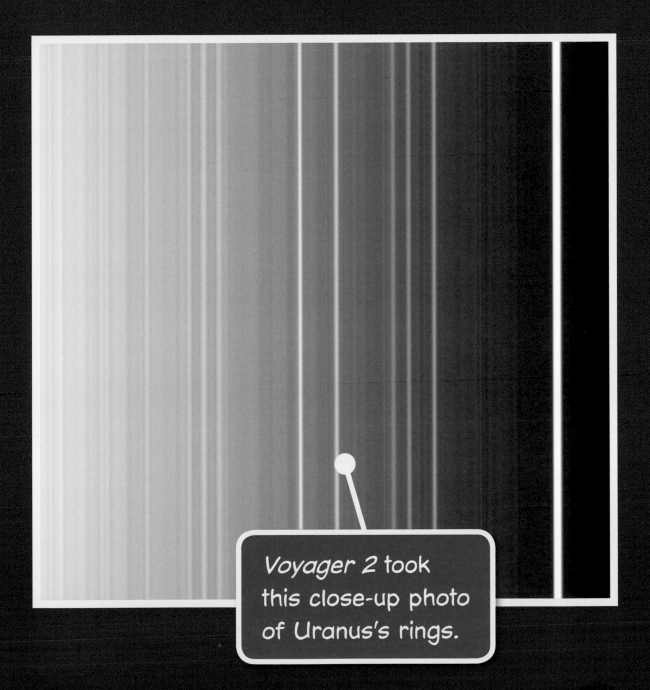

Voyager 2 took this close-up photo of Uranus's rings.

# Living on Uranus

Living things need water to survive. Uranus has small amounts of water in its atmosphere but no water on its surface. Astronomers do not believe Uranus can support life.

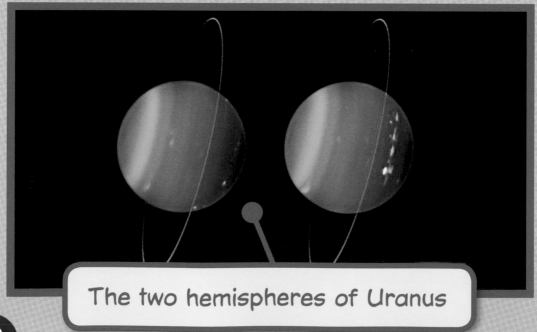

The two hemispheres of Uranus

Uranus is the only planet in the solar system that rotates on its side. It spins the way a ball would if you rolled it on the ground.

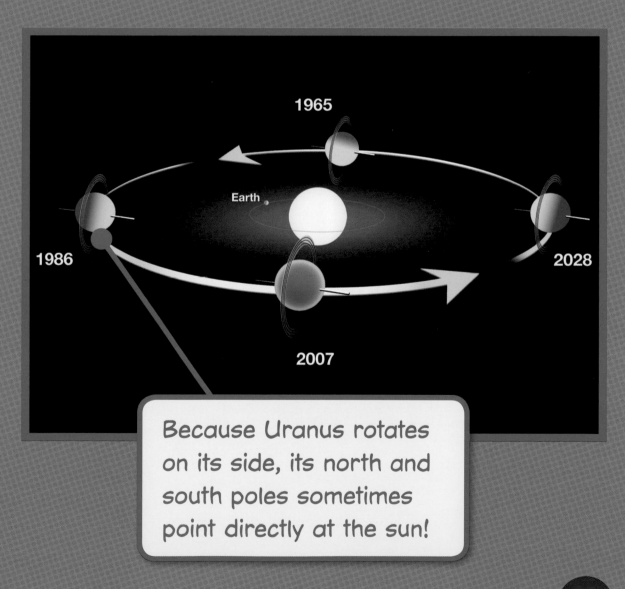

Because Uranus rotates on its side, its north and south poles sometimes point directly at the sun!

How Tilted Are The Planets?

Mercury
0°

Venus
177°

Earth
23°

Mars
25°

Jupiter
3°

Saturn
27°

Uranus
98°

Neptune
28°

This graphic shows how much each planet in our solar system tilts on its axis.

Like Venus, Uranus rotates around its axis in the opposite direction from most planets in the solar system. Astronomers are studying the planets to figure out why.

Uranus has short days and long years. A day on Uranus is about seventeen hours. It takes Uranus eighty-four Earth years to complete one orbit around the sun.

Uranus is the only planet that does not give off more heat than it receives from the sun.

# Checking Out Uranus

Traveling for over nine years, *Voyager 2* became the first spacecraft to visit Uranus. *Voyager 2* studied the planet

for only about six hours, but it uncovered a lot.

Before *Voyager 2* flew by in 1986, astronomers thought that Uranus had only five moons. The spacecraft discovered ten more moons and two more of the planet's rings.

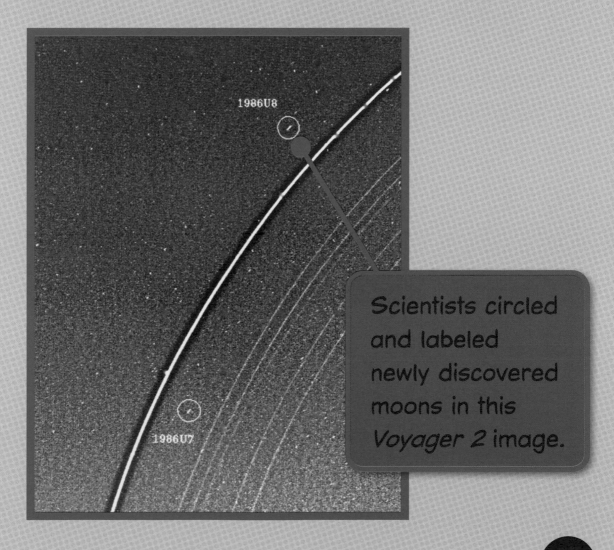

Scientists circled and labeled newly discovered moons in this *Voyager 2* image.

Spacecraft engineers wear special suits and gloves to prevent the spacecraft from getting dirty.

In 2020, scientists looked over *Voyager 2* data and uncovered something new. Uranus released a bubble 22,000 times the size of Earth from its atmosphere. Uranus might release bubbles every time it rotates.

Astronomers plan to uncover more facts about Uranus with the James Webb Space Telescope. The telescope will take photos of Uranus to learn more about the planet.

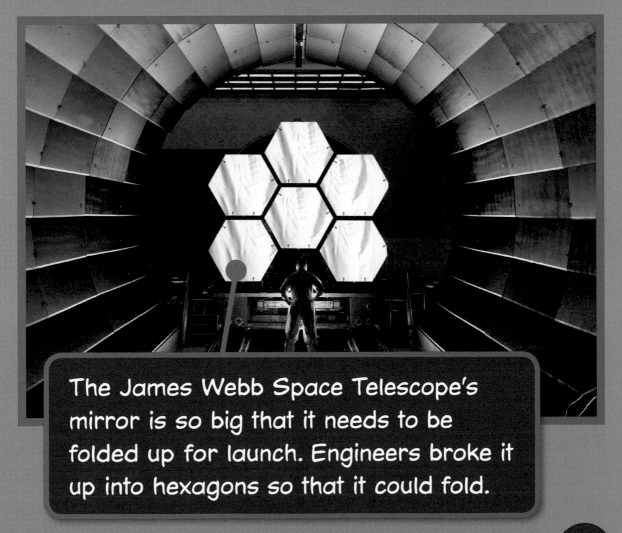

The James Webb Space Telescope's mirror is so big that it needs to be folded up for launch. Engineers broke it up into hexagons so that it could fold.

# Planet Facts

- Uranus gets its blue-green color from the methane gas in its atmosphere. Other gases in the atmosphere make it smell like rotten eggs.

- Uranus may have been knocked onto its side by a long-ago collision with Earth or another planet.

- No spacecraft can land on Uranus because it doesn't have a solid surface. Instead, the planet is mainly swirling gases and liquids.

- Uranus's powerful winds can blast up to 560 miles (900 km) per hour.

# Space Story

Uranus was the first planet to be found with a telescope. William Herschel discovered it in 1781. Herschel originally thought it was a comet or a star. Then another astronomer, Johann Elert Bode, made observations that revealed Uranus was a planet.

Scan the QR code to the right to see Uranus in 3D!

# Glossary

**atmosphere:** the air that surrounds a planet

**axis:** an imaginary line that a planet turns around

**ice giant:** a large, cold planet that has an icy core

**moon:** an object that travels around a planet

**orbit:** a curved path that an object makes as it travels around something else

**ring:** a circle of dust and icy or rocky pieces around a planet

**rotate:** to move or turn in a circle around an axis

**solar system:** a star and the planets that travel around it

## Learn More

Devera, Czeena. *Uranus*. Ann Arbor, MI: Cherry Lake, 2020.

Kiddle: Uranus Rings Facts
https://kids.kiddle.co/Rings_of_Uranus

Milroy, Liz. *Explore Venus*. Minneapolis: Lerner Publications, 2021.

Murray, Julie. *Uranus*. Minneapolis: Abdo Zoom, 2019.

NASA Space Place: All about Uranus
https://spaceplace.nasa.gov/all-about-uranus/en/

# Index

# Photo Acknowledgments

Image credits: NASA/JPL-Caltech, pp. 4, 16, 18; WP/Wikimedia Commons (CC BY-SA 3.0, p. 5; NASA, pp. 6, 9; Mevan/Shutterstock.com, p. 7; NASA/ARC, pp. 8, 10, 17; NASA/JPL, p. 11; NASA/JPL/Lawrence Sromovsky/University of Wisconsin-Madison/W.W. Keck Observatory, p. 12; NASA/ESA/M. Showalter, p. 13; NASA/JPL-Caltech/Richard Barkus, p. 14; janez volmajer/Shutterstock.com, p. 15; NASA/MSFC/David Higginbotham, p. 19.

Cover: forplayday/Getty Images.